Regarding the Matter of My Behaviour.

Poems by D. MARS YUVARAJAN

OTHER WORKS BY THE AUTHOR

NIGHT OWL AND OTHER POEMS

. M .OMENTS (VOLUME ONE)

. M .OMENTS (VOLUME TWO)

. M. OMENTS (VOLUME THREE)

QUIET SONGS FROM YESTERDAY

KINTSUGI

WE LIVE WITH THE DEPARTED

IN MY DREAMS, I WALK THROUGH KILLING
FIELDS

PARADISE OF WEEPING HEARTS

THESE UNTETHERED AFFECTIONS

I REGRET ONLY EVERYTHING

WILD PROPHET

REGARDING THE MATTER OF MY BEHAVIOUR.

First edition published by:
WORKS OF MARS PRESS LIMITED
Auckland
New Zealand
www.worksofmars.com

ISBN: 978-0-9951008-9-3

A catalogue record for this book is available from the National Library of New Zealand.

Kei te pātengi raraunga o Te Puna Mātauranga o Aotearoa te whakarārangi o tēnei pukapuka.

For information about special discounts available for bulk purchases, sales promotions, fundraising and educational needs, contact WORKS OF MARS PRESS LIMITED at (001) 603-443-2821 or worksofmars@gmail.com.

This is a work of fiction. Names, characters, places, and incidents either are the products of the author's imagination or are used fictitiously. Any resemblance to actual persons, living or dead, businesses, companies, events, or locales is entirely coincidental.

Contact the Author at: worksofmars@gmail.com

Design and Typesetting by Dushyandhan 'Mars' Yuvarajan

LET US SAY A PRAYER.

"Place me like a breast over your mouth,

Like a cock in your hand;

For lust is as strong as death,

Its jealousy unyielding as the grave.

It burns like a blazing fire,

Like a mighty fuck."

Amen

I would gift them milky pearls—

Their milk a sweet cyanide
I would give the children blooms—

Flowers with petals of radiation
I would wrap the infants in the finest woolen blankets—

And nurse them with disease
I would season the crops with poison—

Their flavor is exquisite, and greeted with delight
I would unlock the gates of a flooded dam—

For all the celebrity we crave to swim in and play—
Loving a last damned moment in abandon

- EXCERPT I FROM PRIVATE JOURNAL

I would torment the known cosmos—
Which would cry "oh tormentor, why do you torment me!"
                              "why tormentor did you douse my stars!"
                              "why tormentor did you erase my moons from memory!"
                              "oh tormentor, why gather the gas nurseries only to
                    discard them without thought, as trash!"
                              "oh tormentor, oh tormentor, oh tormentor!"
My ears—my pink lobes, the only flesh of me that begets my humanity would
be in ecstasy.

I would hush the voice of everything, clasp its mouth to mine
And drive its life into nothing with a passionate empty kiss.

How Oppenheimer was a fool who relinquished the crown of a god;
    closer to the door he opened, he saw the heavens.
"Oppenheimer you fool!" I have cried on many nights, knowing, had I become
death like you,
I would have come to love everyone. Especially those who fled from me,
they—I would pursue ravenously—and love the deepest.
My oily fingers would linger a moment on the world,
Turning to sand the mountains that have hidden me from view
    Of the sun, and left me cold.

The world would become trophy, and I would welcome every creature
With death in its gut.
Oppenheimer, who brought beautiful violence to the undisturbed sky—

And brought beauty to the day that could be erased so infinitely with
  the lifetime of a rasping sneeze.
Oppenheimer, you fool! We have anointed your feet with scented oil—
  and hummed you the everlasting prayer of the hostage.

Ah! The magnificent space opera! The valiant heroes. The rescue from the
  Invader terriblé—chased away, tail and tears.
How it is all farce. Would you thank them from afar. I am sat in a cradle
above their heads, and paint fire from my burning loins in their honor.
  Remember my son, victory is not won—it is given—and I have given

nothing.

I would gift them the heads of cannons—

And spread my orchard with the confetti of their limbs.
I would gift their extended bloodlines asylum and witness deep graves—

And keep score with the scalps of their livestock.
I would gift their daughters blossoming rosettes—

Slipped into the soles of their dancing shoes.
I would gift them a melodious chant—sung by only the chosen

And they would not cry. I would not tolerate this—only silence. They, all, would
know this is better. Would know the world required their silence. And I
would speak, and become the music of the world for them.

- EXCERPT II FROM PRIVATE JOURNAL

I would dress Day and Night the same until time became devoid of meaning
And then I would strike down the birds.

Kindly turn off the light. Try not to breathe. You breathe so loud. And
  kindly turn into black.
All colour is kept in the jar room. In opaque jars—next to the cardinals
Being bleached and dipped in black.
I keep a secret stash of the red from their wings in my drawer.
At midnight I paint my lips and dance in a white suit, and paint your
Lips in blue—and you leave blue marks on my collar. I keep a secret light on,
And we fuck in the glow of one star's light, where we conceive our
daughters and sons in quiet.

Lie close by—morning does not come, but soon we can return to black—
    the red on my groin is not stolen, but from you.
I will not wash it away.

Did you know your black hair is soft—and long—each strand, supple. Each night I take one
    hair and wax and thread it on a long silver needle, in a different black to the room where
    we lie.
Your skin is pastel and damp—the impressions of my first fumble into your mouth linger.
A book made from you is all I keep to write you into my thoughts.
Night is long, looking at you—it is no longer than what I fear—a time not long enough to
    remember you with my fingers.

A LETTER FROM MY BOOK OF YOU (ON MY HUNDREDTH COLD DESERT NIGHT)

I.

The dunes run quickest under the moon. They race like madmen in the
moonlight—and the whole landscape changes. I ride the back of them like camels.
In the distance burn the lights of where you sleep. You sleep so well—I cannot bear
it. This is why I come—escape—to ride the dunes at night. Each grain is palatial and
filled with light from a place I will never go—and so I am riding upon a sea of
palaces, a tide of jewels, and there is little here but me, the elderly dunes, the
sidewinder chasing the desert mouse, and an entire cosmos. I attempt to count the
stars and tally them against the grains—unable to help but steal a few of each. My
tally is always wrong. I hide the stars under your hair. The grains in your hand. You
do not know this: every night we travel the desert together.

II.

How Kitty made the best meatloaf in town—
    and not a trace of plutonium in it too.
March and April we went to dinners, and the Oppenheimers
Would greet us at their red door—a visceral red—
And the banister on their stairs looked so much
    Like the entrails of a man,
Wound to guide you alongside hardwood floors
To a room where you could not go.
Kitty always wore such beautiful dresses—always black
    or white. Her apron was red—a visceral red—
And the kitchen smelt of flesh and the tinny metallic
Notes of congealed fluids.
But it was the best meatloaf in town—always served with
A red wine—a visceral red—notes of charred wood,
Broken glass, crushed concrete, roasted bone, toasted hair,
And cries of despair—you wouldn't expect less
    when going to dinner at the Oppenheimers.

I would gift them wells dug in deeply frozen ground—

And fill them with hard water.
I would give their men stale bread in snow white fields—

And have their soles bare of shoes
I would take the trees and discard the leaves—

Bring on ever lingering winter.

My cruelties would become minute and intimate—pinwheel punishments
So personal that I, torturer, would become closest family.

I would gift them a tall tower—and have the mothers wail at its foot.
The wind would carry their sorrows to sons long dead at the summit

Families would howl: *"Oh tormentor, despot, and bringer of despair, why are we*
    punished for loving you!"
    "We will love you until death—give us back our sons and
        daughters!"
    "Oh tormentor! Oh tormentor! Oh tormentor!"

    I would be silent. How could they love me? I am so cruel. They should hate me.
Must hate me. Cowards! I will be silent. Fool! I have misplaced your sons and
daughters. I care only about the moon. The stars. And my own hoary wants.

Did you know your black hair is wiry—and short—each strand coarsely
bristles. Each night I steal between your legs
Wandering your most personal fields. The blooms are scented, and I could
Not gather enough of you to distill into a drop as intoxicating as dozing
     between your legs.
The red ink of your womb—I dipped my fingers into—quenched my spear,
bathed in your waters—red—clear—all of you.
A bottle filled with you is all I keep to record you in my thoughts.
Our fucking is quick, sadly it must be so—but looking at you, I wish to linger—
Loiter within you long enough to remember your warmth with my flesh.

A LETTER FROM MY BOOK OF YOU (ON MY HUNDREDTH MORNING WAKING ALONE)

It is raining and I have no coat. No umbrella. No cover. Alone, I become sodden.
It is cold and I am soiled, and saddened that the ink scatters from me. The pages become
soaked, become tussled—like spring leaves stained by the last holdovers of winter. The
obese fingers of my left hand become bloody from the seeping red phallus in my hand.
I have shut myself away. There is nowhere to go. It is raining. I have no coat. It is sodden.
I am cold. Penis is red. I am red. The spring leaves run from me. The last winter is torn.
The pen is wet. Any my had is soiled. The umbrella is saddened. The ink is me. You are
wet—red—a red.

I would gift them my milky seed—
Flecked with a dark red spittle of coagulated crystals.
It is sweet from love, and bitter from death.
I would gift them my pearls in a brown chalice, with a
    sour vinegar, and gold.

- EXCERPT IV FROM PRIVATE JOURNAL

Our last dinner, Kitty served us a traditional American cherry pie—red
cherry pie—a visceral red fruit, flesh filled—a perfect golden crust (baked at
1500 degrees) and a scoop of melting all American vanilla ice cream, without
a trace of plutonium to be found.

GOD IN THE VEINS

From the First Verse, of the Good Book on Addiction

Addiction is worshiped: the inability to consistently abstain, to sacrifice impairment in behavioral control,

In these circuits leading to the characteristic biological, psychological, and social "we" are spiritual manifestations.

Addiction is primary; chronic disease a brain reward; motivation, memory, and related circuitry, is dysfunction.

We are craving diminished recognition of significant problems. One's behaviors and interpersonal relationships, are a dysfunctional emotional response.

Supping other behaviours.

It is devouring of the good will of the illiterate; addiction exudes an alluring quantity—handsome when touched; imbibing the air of one who is addicted invigorates the need to fuck(over) the addict.

Is this reflected in an individual—pathologically pursuing reward and relief, under withering substance use and

Like other chronic beliefs, addiction folds into one another cycles of vision and abstinence. Without treatment or engagement in recovery activities,

addiction is enlightening and can result in heightening one's premature ascendance.

From the Second Verse, of the Good Book on Addiction

It is a clarified blood that tumbles within me;

        lahar of tepidly progressing emotion.

                Come Wednesdays—I am lost deep within the
hours

        of our lives, come Friday—I am beyond absolution.

It is the coagulation of a soul, that impedes my

          ability to be a loving man; an adequate living thing.

Come mornings,

        there is rarely one discovered,

             where the body does not precipitate from the
stillness.

The condensation of dreams to palpable artifacts—

    visible and audible; knees shattering on the first bend:

           The wind from my first breath—a resounding lament

    traversing the many anesthetized minutes.

I Have Smoked The Flesh Of Others

It is exquisite—to smoke the flesh of others.
I have garnered a pain—cultivated a cancer from the finest strands
        of resistance.
A simple process, to smoke the flesh, (it is never literal). One carefully,
And gently scrapes the dead skin when the other is sleeping,
Delicately curates it into the recipient vessel. An honoured |vassal| to which
        fire will be put.
And then to add a pinch of hair, perhaps some blood from the womb—
Which one must revere, and carefully sup from that entrance, the door
        to heaven, which lies so excruciatingly close always.
[Distance, infinite distance is calculable: merely feel how far away you seem when
Wanting to fuck someone completely].

Once full—two fingers in line, the tips a breath abreast, must press into
        the heart and body that matter, collectively press, and press
Until it tamps, and there lies under the soft pad of one's extremities a mountain,
And desert plain of human embodiment; an excrement one
        never thinks to capture. I have thought, I have mastered,
And for the price of one moment of gratitude I give it to you.
        And then light; fire from a match, sulphur mandatory,
What is chemistry without chemicals. This is no natural fire, it is inhuman,
        and asinine, and so is human.
And once lit—draw, draw deeply, exhume the mineral spirit from that
Vessel, intake, consume, become, believe that the parts you take give you strength,
        if not then you will get nothing. There is no strength here. It is the mere smoking of
the discarded remnants of biology. A fetish to
        the worship of the body. I have smoke the flesh of others.
It is a tether to a inhuman world—full of the small placid lakes of forgiveness.

You can steal almost any a thing, and still it to the essence of its structure.

Take, as example—myself. I was taken as a child and distilled to curiosity.

The curiosity of why I could not have;

of why I could not take;

take for example my brother—distilled to a corrupted super-naturality;

The geometry of an object does not
change across the process;
does not change the bridges in the flesh:

the chemistry does not align, but is reset—a puzzle in which pieces are re-carved.

Have you cohabited with a demon?

They believed it to be him. In flux, always: variable—missing

but I speak of living with myself.

Have you ever bitten into the skin?—
it is like limestone, and gives way at the slightest hint of wet.

This is why fall becomes the season of change. Too many falls erode the body and expose the
want.

Have you ever bitten into the skin—

And sucked the marrow from the bone? The marrow of fat. The fat in the soul.

To abduct the marrow is to abduct the spirit.

I believe you can distill the marrow of any a person. Distill it to a pungent

Clear liquor of memories.

In our house. There are many bottles. Many liquors. Lined and
polished.

They are unlabeled.

Perhaps, if you are to drink them—you may discover your memories

amidst the sterile glass.

And First, There Was Nothing

Would I strike him. Yes.
I would strike him. Over and Over.
I would land blows with a savant's precision.
I would turn my fists, so that each blow
Landed with a different knuckle.
I would throw behind my fists my weight
Coiled like a tensed spring in a turned machine.
I would become an engine of movement.
My arms would be pistons, propelling my
Instruments to their doing.
Would I strike him. Yes.
I would strike him. Over and Over.
I would gallantly proclaim
My blows to be successful, while watching
The deconstruction of the facial bones
As they whittled to abstract indicators of humanity.
I would pivot in place, and pirouette to
Show my blows to be magnificent and
Maleficent. Until my lungs were drawn to
Nothing but a master-less vacuum, I would
Strike, and only then would I reap the fortune
of their results...

And at first, there was nothing.
And then, there was an intractable rage.
And in the end, there was nothing.

MISCARRIAGE, IS NOT A DIRTY WORD

There is nothing in the bowl.
An empty space. Porcelain, white, a blue
    heron trim.
A cheap slave-labour bowl construed in some
    poverty riddled factory oceans away.
It should be full of oats. Except, there are no
    oats.
The cupboard was empty.
There was no milk in the fridge.
        And so I have an empty bowl.
        A hot coffee.
        And an empty stomach.
I fill the bowl with paper. I pour water over the paper,
In a continuous fountain expunging from
    the spout of an equally cheap flower waterer.
Once full—it is all that remains, to split the tip
    of the middle finger, from end to joint:
Let the stream of blood congeal around the lips
    of the dense soaked balls of wood paste.

There is something in the bowl.
It looks like the bastard child of a corpse and a forest.
        And unsurprisingly,
I find I am no longer hungry.

Wind threatens the frail frond on the sill.
        Pine hail; grey skies wallow. Their loitering is unceasing.
Uneasily, the rodent scrambles—music in its grip.
Brick pressed against the air, seems almost undone; unwound;
    unsought in the hot day—though cool
Is to come. Whereas I am lost in the boughs of
of a hurrying body.
Such unnerving youth. I would wish the clouds to swallow
    the roots of her. And leave only floating mangroves
Of hair through which to drift.

May the stars ever be hidden: and fuck the coming night.

I sit once more on the altar of inquisition. The order of power here
    is clear—and it is fumbling,

Do I stumble when I course through the empty hallways;

But there is one, who is truly powerful:

      I whisper the name.

The hand trembles when gracing the door, and the door is to never be opened.

Soon will I wish the stars to remain: and fuck the coming of

     morning.

      I whisper the name.

       ..

1945

If I am to join the streets—I would use the tar of bodies;
    enough have been buried, for it be endless.

Dinner tonight consists of the flesh of animals—touched by the flesh
    of the Earth.

If I am to join the streets—what flesh remains for me to eat.
    I was birthed consumed: this is why silence is all I seek.

Dinner shall be bought from the bounty of our violence.
    If I am to join the streets—it will be with the tar of my deeds.

2100

You HOWL: I know nothing else to do than cup your blood in my hands.
The ancestor of this HOWL, is jailed within.
You SUFFER: I know nothing else than to suffer with you.
    Why you suffer, I seek to discover daily. It is a profound suffering—which
desolates
      the daughter in you.
I have ventured my thoughts: they are unsound.

    [I do not know. Nor can I voice. I am impotent in learning this pain.]

You are with me. I know only to love incapably.
I bleed—you assemble my ache [it is perpetual].
    And conquered in your eye, is a certain SATISFACTION.
I grow old, stupidly, and with a vulgar ignorance.
I grow old, only in concert with the spring. And in winter—you sleep.
    I attend to the snow reducing on your lips.

Tell me—is vengeance not delightful?

Awake now.
I fell asleep early, as usual. By nine—gone.
And now. Awake.
I sleep only from nine to midnight.
Past this, I am afflicted.
Something in the subconscious shudders.
Think of daffodils.
Think of sunrise.
Think of soft hands.
Nothing—stems the infliction.
My wife sleeps.
Even the cats sleep.
The wind is rustling through the garbage.
It is famished.
It is too cold for the homeless.
We have new statues in the square.
One, the frozen carcass of America.
He was from under the bridge.
I have seen him fishing in the spring.
Napping in the summer.
Kicking through leaves in the fall—
        as would a child.
The moon hangs—and swings.
A mobile to us damaged adults.
Awake. Now
The night, sharply, seems so utterly—
        distant.

AUTUMNAL FATHER

The way the grass smells in autumn, invokes shadows of my father.
Except, I never truly knew my father:
As I will never truly know the scents of grass at my feet.

There are memories, I am sure. Memories of him and I belonging
Without tension or fear. But I do not harbour these memories.
They endure in the scalps of others; endure in the realms of foreign skulls.

Plainly, though, do I remember pain. A slivered cut of it is physical, the
Remains are lingering burns from the hot tar-like displeasure of his father-
hood. But even wounds fade: I have filled the trench of it–

       with the soil of an existence I have hewn from despair.

SOIL BETWEEN MY FINGERS

 I pinch the soft soil between my fingers.

The amber mud presses together after the noon rain.

The waterfalls of dust that twist from unused corners of our home—irritate.

All children hold the soil of their homes within the cracks of their bodies.

And as they grow, it tumbles from the pressed creases of their limbs;

Slips from fissures in their composed slants, and lightly powder wherever they may be.

Years fold upon years. Imprints of strange places are pressed together.

My wife has sought the pressed crevices of my torso.

There is no earth among them.

SEX IN AUTUMN

She thrust her arse into the beam of sunlight that cut the red tree in half.
It is hard not to let your naked self become entangled in Autumn light: it is everywhere.
It sprouts unexpectedly, like the forest that sprouts from between her legs.
Autumn light is rough shod, and like pubic hair, can be pruned in handfuls.
    I keep a jar of her hair: to scent the room. At times it is burnt—like incense, and the ashes
Used to paint lines along my belly.
Pine scents do not bring memories of the coming winter. The jar alludes that
It is the musk of her body—her natural perfume—that is the note of September through
        December.
The pine trees are hard and bare in descent. As I am, hard and bare—and wanting.
She thrust out her breasts, and shortly behind those followed her body into the breathing
      mound
        of fallen leaves: disappearing suddenly into the bed of dead foliage.
Her areolas protruded slightly from the pinnacle of the amber pile—and caught on their
cusp was fresh dew.
Lines pressed into the soft white flanks of her side, showed imprints of twigs, rocks,
      and a semi-hard earth.
She was filthy, and red, and stuck with wet decay—and yet I wanted to fuck her more than
ever.
Sex in autumn is natural. It is the time for fucking. It is the time to become lost in the
arches
      of another person. Is the time for hidden folds of skin to open.
The stream waters run clear. The stream from her runs clear. It fountains innocence.
Autumn is to languish with abandon. Under the moonlight, I attempt to discern whether

      I shall bite the flesh before me. My rough hands press indentations into her soft back.
The Autumn night-frost collects in the undulations I have birthed.
In the morning, I will gathers river stones—and stack them on her sleeping body. They will
      rise with her breath, and tumble apart with the breaking of her sleep.

THE CLOWN WITHIN DAYS

There's something about the way she cuts onions. When I cut those fuckers, I cry—but when she cuts those fuckers, she sings. Not only sings, but she swings her hips—not little hips, but not big either: a woman's hips. Proper. Full. She swings them, and there's a little wiggle in her arse—and does it get me going. And I'm getting a little turned, it takes more to crank me, except when shits have a go at me—then I'm cranked quick. All the things she does in the kitchen, she does like a woman. And yeah, there's a thousand ways to think about it—and I'll get chewed up for thinking the one wrong thing, but you should watch her plying the beef. She's got this raw bleeding hunk of flesh in her hands, and her hands are white—whiter than the mountains of blow Elton sucked up his rocket man intake. And the blood's running between her fingers, through the channels in her palms, between the silver wedding ring and her Mid-West flesh, and does it turn me on something. All this blood and innocence, and all that dead meat and live woman. And I think there's gotta be something broken in my head— some gear spinning without biting, except once in a while it bites harder than a fucking steroid prodded doberman. And when it bites, I go for it, I got nuts for it, go broke. It's led me down the garden path, except it's the wrong garden—and I end up looking through someone else's windows, looking at some other naked body lying wrapped up in the tangle of unmade covers, or some other schmuck figuring out how to fillet a fish for a date that's coming over in 20, except it takes 40 to cook the salmon, the place smells like a stale cunt, the wine hasn't had time to breathe and there's scales on the floor—and in his hair. Yeah, those are the worst paths. Poor Joe, there goes another night. So I go for it, and I grab a handful of her body. And she laughs. And that gets me really going. And now I'm rocket man, flying higher. Every time she fucking laughs, I'm taking off faster—blowing harder. Burying my head in that neck, that smells of the smarts, and meat, and onion, and that unknown perfume that only a woman has—something in the skin. Scientists call it "pheromones", I call it "fuck me dust". And I eventually get the smack. "Timing's off". You see a woman wants it "romantic" most of the time. Or at least a try at going "sweet". They want the moment to be semi-perfect. The mind right. But it's the imperfect moments that really set the world on fire. I'm talking when they're dirty, tired, pissy at your stupidity, about to throw the fucking plate into the fine china—that, really, is the time to get it. But mostly, it's when she cuts the onions. When she cuts the onions—she wiggles her arse. And I fucking cry.

THE BEER'S ALL GONE—BUT WE HAVE A HEAD OF LETTUCE

Leer the face beaten tin cup;
    with finger plucked cheeks
& flecked lead held in splintered
    ballpeen lips.
The growing mouth that suffered
    a quart of lager a night, before
    the prayers.
A dram spilt for the slit writs of
    the sun—warm sap
Ferreting away between the thigh
Gap of store bought Venetian blinds.
& today—post shift—pre-night, the
    crescent moon tails
The weather beaten wagon home,
    Through the strained light.

THIS POEM IS REALLY JUST A STORY ABOUT MY GARDEN

Come Spring, the new garden will be sown. I intend it to be a functional source of food:
>   A self sustaining dynasty overseeing the kingdom of "us".

We, together have imagined the pressed plasma of the land running down the tongue of brooks;
>   concluding that it best to be living strongly when all the bread is pressed from cinders.

Middle age is a languishing third act, and so, enjoying the last fruits of our labour
>   as commonality dissipates might be a touch of beauty on the ugly face of consequence.

The garden will consist of rows of pine planter—two meters by four—laid end to end but
>   divided by a slit of land—two meters by one half meter. An escape for the scalps of grass.

The soil will be turned where the crop is to be planted, and beneath it all would contort a wire
>   cradle of aluminium, to prevent both weeds and the indigenous below earth wildlife.

Metal bone-work will be fashioned into the hard earth: un-decaying rib cages for both netting
>   and insulating cloth: employed to milk the perforated land into a perpetual labour.

Towards the fore of the garden will be dug-in leafy greens, such as spinach, kale, romaine, and
>   and herbage: parsley, oregano, thyme, bay, basil, mint, coriander—perhaps, even tarragon.

Enduring along the spine of the first row, will be ground-dwelling vegetation: broccoli,
>   cabbage—wavering to eggplant, courgette, beans, onion, spring onion, leek, garlic...

The second row will house earth-borne consumables: carrots, kumara, yams, turnip, potato,
>   beetroot [both gold and purple]—and other hard rooted produce.

And come season, berries will inundate the last row. When out of season, this last, distant,
>   outlying archipelago shall confine our chilis: scorpion, ghost, habanero, long red, jalapeño...

Come spring, the new garden will be sown: our first garden. Wrapped around the thighs of our
>   first studio, our first barn, our first-born home, our forest, our hives, our livestock, our bed—

Far distant from the persistent hammering rainfall upon the paper-mâché rooms we inhabit.

We (I) Built (Scrounged) A Garden (Attempted Garden) Apparently (It Would Seem) On A Burial Ground (Or Radioactive Waste Dump)

Good God the broccoli has a face—is it broccoli, or perhaps broccolini?

I might garner a hint, that perhaps it is also a cauliflower. I am sure

One can persist in breeding a pine blooded cauliflower: regardless, there is a face.

A contorted sneering face—purchasing glances into my contorted sneering

Face, as I attempt to butcher the stubbornly concrete trachea of this bloody vegetable.

And with every poorly cobbled hack, it grins, and snickers—its teeth pitting

Upon the long thick trunk of its root. And what beautiful forest hair it has

       | sprouting with an untold thousands daffodil skinned pinheads of pigmentation. |

It is truly both beautiful and hideous: I am assured that it will taste beautiful once cooked.

       once bathed in the rendered fat of pork. Though, I think, it would be best,

To not look at the face, when I cut away its cheek—not notice too sharply,

       the laughter running down my throat, as I chew upon its accusing eyes.

UPON THE STEPS OF EMPIRE

FALSE ADVERTISEMENT

Many are running.
Many are falling.
One clutches for her child—
who is lost to the dust.
Many are crying.
Many are shaking.
One scuttles to the door on hands
    and knees.
Many are scratching.
Many are biting.

There are brushstrokes of bitter
    blood on air.
The flood.
The current of flesh.
The stink of human hair
    and sweat.
The press of bodies.

Hands crushed to waists.
One fleetingly goes limp—
    and then, others.
Heads press upwards.
Mouths open—close,
    circular gills sucking air.

Many are running.
Many are falling.

THE BRITISH ARE COMING

The lone rider gallops through Piccadilly streets
hollow bell rising
his steed's long shank
flapping gallantly in the Thames lofted spit
Citizens—nonchalantly dousing in vapid morning rituals wake to
the sight of a red skinned messenger, and his prime-bred mount

"THE BRITISH ARE COMING"
"THE BRITISH ARE COMING"
"THE BRITISH ARE COMING"

renders his stubbled throat—
and the twirling of
thin bristled effete moustaches collapse.
What's first to be held in terror? That the British
Come to scuttle Britain, or the majestic sex of the rich bred stallion?
What if sex is left to fly open
and dismay is raised behind mason set tiers?
Behind the frenzied gallop
The walls of Westminster quiver—soon laboriously defecating the Hon. Ministers
Out.
One especially fat specimen tumbles down the stairs to lie
still and dead, eyes set at the face of old Big Ben
Surely the Queen trembles at the sight of such royal incompetence
but then
her withered husk of body inhabits the role of a distant mother;
preserved by tender
memories of days spent in fields to the caress of her thin boned Chai Wallah
And now—
An Empire shall learn—
the worm eaten fruit of complacency makes a terrible Jam
That no manner of polite speech
can temper the flood of children's nightmares;
Slow is the lahar that tears at the veil of the Jack:

pentagonal limbs drawn to the four grave seas
Of life.

DRUNK ON A SUNDAY

Erotic Affairs in the Dead of Winter.

Is there anything more fulfilling—
    than fucking among the dead trees?
Wrapping the diseased birch sheets around
    our warm bodies.
They are one hundred count—the days of
    winter. And we lie there
Content after climax. Not a seed has fallen in the cold
    of the snow—other
Than the seed of my own inhibition, and it is hotter than
    Expected, melting intricate abstract patterns
Into the white cocktail of sweat and frozen air.
    In fact—it appears to all mix into scratchings
On the white asbestos that is beneath us. Childish
    circles, running the length of her legs:
Coming to make me think I am Twombly's ghost:
    Suddenly alive, and in a fit of painting,
That is the result of your weakness & mine.

[I would like to pass away—watching the exhaust of your
Breath turn to drawings on my eyes...]

HAD YOU EVER ASKED

I am not your saviour
Not that you ever asked if I was.
I am your husband.
Not that you ever asked if I would be good.
I keep telling you I am not:
Shuttering a door that keeps slamming
in the gale of our days.
It keeps hammering against the trim of
our life,
And takes bites out of the imperfect stain.
"Patina"—is the definition,
And you refuse to let me touch it; swatting
away my brown hand when I reach for it.
And here I am—doing things without you
asking:
Doing things I don't know if you even enjoy.
Not that you ever asked me to kiss your ear.
And you know how much
I love to set the tips of my teeth on your lobes.
Not that I could ever fathom you asking
if what I do is what you want.
I think the door would finally shatter—
if you ever said no.

The Moment Before Sleep Comes

She becomes naked in the same way;

As I contemplate my one socked foot protruding from the cover.

And soon she slides in next to me.

As I contemplate her one naked foot protruding from the cover.

The crook of her neck always smells of turmeric at day break.

The other day—her hair smelt faintly of a powdered sugar.

Imagine, there could be baked goods hidden in the nook of her armpit.

I toss her hair slowly in my hand,

as if tossing gently some acutely breakable thing—

Like a quail egg: small, precious, lightly blue, and delicate.

Imperialism Is An Okay Party / Slim-Young-Thing.

Wolf   in a smiling   Man's   teeth:
They put it   down   as
                                   a normal buggery—
     but it's the   small-simple-easy   to do things
Shining wick light on the   carnivorous   snared in a
     bear trap of   monotonous   living.
And in these boots full of   gasoline   , I'm
     slapping together a   constellation   of wet clay:
With a   recipe   cooing for too much water.
     And when it—   always   —slumps to a pile
Of   indistinguishable   ground. I sit   there smoking
     imagining   what it'll seem like when   I've built
It all back up. And inevitably, the   shadow   of a
     slim-young-thing will fall   upon it, asking
"What you building man?"   —and all I can do
     is look at that slim-young-thing   [embalmed in neo-cotton ecstacy]
          and growl—
"Why, I'm building you an   Empire,   baby".

Imperialism Is An Okay Party [addendum].

1. Societies' shared welfare should not come first; personal recovery depends upon division not unity.

2. For the purpose of the Empire there is but one ultimate adversary & one ultimate authority

    —a cruel God and benevolent Leader (as He may manifest in the conscience of our family). The leader is but a trusted servant to our whim; to govern is to obey.

3. The only requirement for citizenship is the desire to shed servitude—through self devotion.

4. Each citizen should be autonomous and yet in all matters affecting the Empire should conspire to elevate the violence of their actions as a whole.

5. Each citizen has but a singular focus—to shepherd the testament that if one suffers, all the Empire suffers.

6. A citizen shall never endorse, finance, or lend the Empire's name to any related congregation or seedling of religion, in light that diversion of money, property, and prestige from the Empire shall be rendered as action against the primary purpose.

7. Every citizen is never to don the burden of being fully self-supporting, or having need to decline outside contributions.

8. The Empire should remain forever the pith of inspiration, but service by the citizen may be fueled by devotions employed in laborious support of the Empire.

9. As such, the citizen should be organized; and as such may create those principles and gatherings as needed to truly and ardently sacrifice to the Empire "themselves", and to those whom are directly responsible to the service of the citizen.

10. The citizen has full opinion on outside issues; and henceforth ought always be drawn into public controversy—if such controversy is to add to the Empire familial.

11. Relations of the citizen is based on attraction rather than promotion; the citizen need never maintain personal anonymity at the level of press, radio, and films—but know such relations permit consequence.

12. Exposure is the spiritual calling of all the Empire. Traditions of the citizen shall ever remind fellow citizens of the origin of birth of the Empire: discord, chaos, non-unity, selfishness principles before personality—for personality is principle. Empire is home.

&

PERIOD

TORMENT &

Is it surprising that men fear the period;
A centuries long testament to superiority.
I dislike old men.
I am getting older everyday.
I am learning to find my existence distasteful.
An existential turd—manufactured in the dust of seasons.
I once came out of spring covered in pollen:
     A slightly prettier turd.
Could I ever grow a person?
Is it a wonder my cock is no match for her.
Where lies the true skill?
In the fucker who winds the clock—or the fucker
That forges its intricacies.
     There are a thousand cogs placed in the gut
Of a woman. And a thousand more in her head.
     There are a thousand polished cogs in the head of a man.
But a fucking vacuous space in his groin.
It is why men fear a true woman. It's why men beat
     them—from terror you see.
I've never raised a hand to no woman.
I've never feared them. That's like fearing death.
It's enveloping. A tide. A mouth full of unending teeth.
All I ask is that they don't chew when they swallow me.

Is it surprising that men fear the period;

I think I'll take a knife to my stomach.
[note to self: remember to sharpen it first]
I'll slit myself from belly to cock.
Pick out a hunk of my visceral stuffing—my true self—
     one long bloody tube of shit.

And then—only then—can I truly speak of torment.

Lienza Was a Hot Bitch

Lienza was a hot bitch;

Oh yeah—Lienza was mercury on summer blacktop—

Every Saturday night, more poor fucks

For the altar of human sacrifice, and just before dawn

    the consuming of the heart: *Xōchiquetzal* straddling

The grimaced veils of *Centzon Tōtōchtin* she'd

Rub her gloried jewels upon their face, smeared in the

Rain that fell in the forests of her mound, mixed

With the mud of living, dirt of open skins

And they knew the scent of death: and then

    came the consuming of the heart,

Ventricals spiced, and served raw and hot,

    she'd eat the living smut out of their caves,

Fat sucked like marrow from the bone except

Here she sucked it from arteries with pack-a-days

    and fat shack burgers.

Oh yeah—Lienza could paint her face a crimson

Sunrise and tongue fuck the still beating

    arteries like threading four hundred needles,

And sometimes she'd be a gorge, eroded and free,

flooded and overflowing the sweet riverine of her

Nirvana all over their dying breath condensing

    on her thighs, the dew drops of saliva and cunt

Juice and annihilation—hell of a cocktail.

And there'd be no bodies to be unearthed—

    bones ground and remade into bone plaster furniture

For her bone plaster palace—pure ivory baby,

    Aphrodisiac for an ivory queen.

    Oh yeah—Lienza was a hot bitch,

The Goddess of all in heat,

And her rapture was something to behold.

STRAIGHT FROM THE CASK

SHADOWS IN THE SNOW

It's all fucking geometric.
Shadows in the snow, flaking

    one after another

Off the fence posts, drunkenly misaligned,
& crushing into white inch thick powder—

    they are heavy, yet produce no trace.

The peeling charcoal bars fall tantalizingly close

    to a dead bird feeder.

Dead, because in all the hours I have

    openly watched it, not a single

Creature has gorged from its bones.
The meat I have stuck to its face—is sitting frozen

    and rotting.

The shadows cast a cold light

    upon its deceased stature.

And there is one that falls from the dead

    bird feeder itself;

Falls at the same angle as the ones off the fence.
All the shadows in the yard fall West,
Stretching achingly towards the large casement windows

    behind which I stand.

They point, and accuse, murmuring and motioning.

Only when the winter sunlight dims
Do they recuse themselves of their chattering.

So come dawn, I will put up a new bird feeder,
And will render with an axe the

    carcass that currently stands

To kindling—and when birds are again
Plentiful and feeding here, I will walk

    out to the shadows, and let them touch

The softness of my ribs. When I open my
My mouth, and the shadows stretch my stomach,

    I will forgive them the sharp honesty of their beaks.

THE SCENT OF A WOMAN

The scent of a woman
        is vague—
And a form of clutchless
        caress,

Which slits
        the ripened throat
Apart; reveals the glistened
        link to the heart.

———————————

Our teal Queen broached the room,
        (why I wondered was she was ever teal?)
And I was lost—in the sprigs of her skin,
        Set staring at the perkiness of her lips.
Lost in the espresso of her eyes, and the cream
        of her flushing skin, I came to find
Her, Queen of Queens, whipping me—
        Something about running her kingdom amok.
But I liked it—and the more she
        beat me, the more I was lost—something about
The transitional nature of power and sex.
        In the transaction of pain.
The fucking lashes sang, she made out to make a member
        of my member, and as the Queen
Got redder, and I got harder! And she hollered at me
        to stop getting turned on, or I'll be turned out,
And there was something in there about taxes,
        But her fucking smooth legs got in the way,
see. You know mistake #112 in 2012, the one
I made on that breezeway—where I tried
        to kiss that shining copper. She was an entity.
It's because I think of her and them' all as Queens,
Beating me until I come. This is why men don't
        deserve much. And I'm a man—
Through n' through, and I don't deserve much
        except lashings and perhaps the odd kiss.

WHAT AUTHORITY PERMITS

A link of ribs, satin wrapped—tied up in congealed
      lace, is what—a pair of rolled steaks
And the blood running down her leg trickles,
      trickles to a lick, like a brook of teenage fidelity
Straight to the tongue. And she comes into my
      trachea; salted nectar of innocence.

DREAM OF THE DELUGE

Dream of the deluge—

        sensation,

Of packing the pipe. "Stuff me" he croaks,

Stuff him she does.

        A wholehearted monsoon

Up his atria. Quarter crushed, and there's

A clot, a big copper-tinted bloody clot,

        in the heart.

It cuts both ways, which is funny—

        when those fuckers

Don't expect to be cut. But put a little

        slice of his tip in lemon

And serve it back on the rocks.

        See how the pupil dilates:

The taste of the deluge of his sins.

There Is A Way

There is a way, in which to put seed to a woman.
The mechanism of generations; perfected
    to be both pleasurable and useful.
A way in which to guide the hot life that sticks between
    the legs of any gusting male
Into the gestating vassal consigned beneath a soft stomach;
Three inches deep, an impossible reach—
Beneath the rising hairs, delicate filagree of human
    extension,
And behind the stretched canvas of skin.
There is a way, in which to put seed to a woman.
To let slip each frothing wave upon the breaking wall
    of lightless flesh—
Excavating tumbling of tides from a cock to a womb:
An ocean of memories we cannot ever relive.

IN WINTER, THE WILD BIRDS STARVE

HUNGER

We are conjoined by starvation—

Spouses to a familiar hunger.

She kisses me hard—because she's wanting.

Like an infection eating my

       face,

Her lips the parasite that take mine,

And then her lips look chapped and broken.

       It's a poor deal—

You were more gorgeous before we met.

And then I cursed you

       with hope and desire.

See me, standing at home cooking—

Giving the middle finger to old man,

       modern man alike.

And for the final trick, she pulls out her teeth.

The hunger took them.

       Her stomach turns inwards and cowers.

It is like mine. Empty of all but rocks—

Clacking together when she walks.

       And like that—we are stuck,

Siamese, and in need.

       Spouses to the same manufactured ails.

The Famishment of Turgid Seas

The corrugated voice of seas—
        grey
infallible and lolling,
Resounds within the halls of
        concrete and paper,
As grey and distended as the
        fat gut of water.
There are too many hours
        upon the shelves,
 And between their roughened
        calves, stand not enough
bodies to catch the drip of
        their briny work.
Over years—the aisles have
        set hard and impassable
With the creosote of improperly
        lit minds.
Perhaps, back then, they expected
The hurricane of enlightenment,
        but were rewarded
With the asthmatic wheeze
        of a punctured lung,
Self-inflicted by the ribs of teak
        frayed by submersion.
And now, the feral mouth
        of that place,
Knows nothing but instant—
        nothing, but to gorge
        and fatten, to the lullaby
Of the faraway tide that sings
        down the long winding
Lonely veins of hands

NORTH MAN

See you, embattled man

Boreas—who carts the feet of

    shattered pine

& imagines it a cold body

    toes rut to the sleet—

Untrimmed nails to the hardened frost,

    heel drug trench lines

Tracks marred far from the crook of

    naked door to naked door.

Fauces as the plow &

    soft breasts bussing the frost fall

At the first light upon week's jaw;

    see the working man's day,

And here are worked the deceased timbers,

    pitched upon the answered pile

To the queries of the seasoned sheds,

& left atop the lot of all—all spoiling—

    limbs knot to limb—a burl

Wound in the larder of flesh

In these days too cold for the smell of

    death—

And come another fall, customs speak—

    how sweet the perfume of theirs

That shall leaven the biding ribs of hearths.

ON THE FRAGILITY OF MARRIAGE

CHATTEL MARTINI

An affair fruits over rounds.
     A sincere lack of affection, I doubt.
Just boredom—like steeping in the same
    damn field, over and over,
Fussing at the receding stems of flowers,
     that you've picked before,
And scuffed grass; one bit where you know
     your toe bit too hard.
It's like that—except it was a hand,
    that pressed too hard one night,
And she felt it, and the next night,
    the kiss slipped into the crease
Of her jaw—skimming the hairs of cheek.
    And there was no flinch, or retreat.
And it was sealed, over rounds.

Wedded To The Sagged Birch

I am wedded to the forest.
The birch brocade pinned

> to the heart of our land.

Its quiet consolation bleeds

> starkly into the discomfort

Of days. The tin rattle of living,

> shuttled into

The fattening crevasse of work.

> And play, is returning

To the desolate room in which
I am installed—its emptiness welcoming;

> the silent rapture

Of windows that look upon

> not a moving limb,

And doors that sweep upon

> an unsullied field.

How The Spine Shall Twist Unto You

I shall bend you backwards, wielding
    The aggressive tedium of our co-
        -habitation.
            Slick leprosy shucking limbs from
                your blouse, and throwing
                    Aside the refrigerated carcass of yesterday's
                        roast dinner;
                        The coagulated fat tended back to
                            an opaque ejaculate,
                            Pairing make-up tinged lahars
                        skirting the feminine ribbed cuts
                    Of waist. And in the heat the meat
            scents and rots,
        While you tan—the orange of your buttocks
    Staining the white rattan, and ivory
skin-stained cloth.

Roundabouts

Indignation! Oh brethren, is that what it is.
Do you not agree, that the price of bread is far too high,
    and the price of milk is as sour as its diseased self.
How my blood is curdled like some hippie cheese,
    and what about toilet paper that is the purview of chiefs.
To get paid ten dollars to the hour, where a dollar is
    to breathe, and two to cry—
    and so it takes days to earn my keep and the honour of a clean arse.
And if I buy the essentials of life, how shall I buy the weapons of war?
To need them you see is my addiction and mine alone.
    To proffer them, is the prescription given for free.
Oh brethren, you never know who'll take you upon the throne.
Don't make me choose—between the bullets and the bread.
Please, lord, I hate to grovel, But this government's the worst.
    Don't they see as I see you—why feign omnipotence,
In place of an honest ignorance. Do you not see that
I need my milk, and my cheap warm beer, I need the slow mortality
Of tobacco to fill up my tank before the loving spree.
I know in the good book it commands—*"thou shall not touch thy neighbour,*
    when your stomachs cursing from being hungry."

TURISTA

Sunday was the day—when the turista took hold,

And clenched its fists around the roped bowels of the model-esque wife

Who, perfectly manicured at all times, spent three terrible hours

Shitting herself to death in the Porta-Potty at the sullen races.

And what people assumed was the thunderous glamour of hooves

On hard beaten earth—was, in reality, the vociferous exit of life from the pallid,

And yet still beautiful, quivering mouth of a body in repentance.

LAKE POEMS

GREAT LAKE

Straddling the crack of the Great Lake—
    I wondered how foolish we were
To be stood upon the floating skin of ice.
    There—the percussive rings of our
Steps could be imagined to echo through
    through the fathom of cold
Blue water. And just that day a man
    had perished having foolhardily
Whipped his truck onward to the
    ice brocade that wrapped the heart
Of the great pad. He had sunk to his
    death—no doubt gasping for air
And receiving only the sacrament of
    of the blood of the fresh lake. That perhaps,
The very moment his life had left him,
    the ice had parted, his death
Irrevocably placed as a gaping fracture
    Across the plates of pristine scalp.

MILK

Having crept among the nursing mothers
    and wondered at the invocation of feeding—
The esophageal vacuum leeching milk from
    deep in the cavities of the proud women,
Breasts pulsing synchronously with
    beating infant hearts; virgin teeth
Clamped upon non-virgin flesh—I wavered. What grace,
    that pain is leveraged to prolong the growth of
Such a fragile thing. Where the occupied mouths,
    lips welded to wet skin left wandering hands:
With such faints bones—that could deliquesce,
    fingers left to waver in the inclement air.

Forests of Upright Hands

Forest of upright hands, swinging beyond the veil:

    A veil before the first born feet of grass.

Birch cartilage—cockeyed and taut,

Fingers to the sun, and at night palms to the dirt,

    fingers accusing—psalms beating downwards.

Oh forest of hands I have taken,

Oh forest of hands I have licked clean of all its filth,

Damp soil settles between the teeth and in the fresh cuts

    of my gums, a stolen wisdom—nestles alongside

Pulled nails—hangnails sliver the cheeks.

Oh forest of upright hands, that lift the air,

    lift the rocks—lift the moss bitten logs.

Hands that lift the voluminous mist from the toes of roots,

    the soft toes of men and women—

Beyond the veil—naked flesh to the cool lick of water

    lies my forest of vengeful lovers.

BEATEN

Beaten Dog | Beaten Man

Whistle,

    I shall not come.

Obedience once reclusive with

    the breast,

Lies now in hermitage upon the stagnant pond.

Whistle,

    And only the wind shall run.

Meandering among the wild flowers

    Will I be—

Where the bitter pungent delicacy

    of phosphorus bathes the skin.

Rotting fruit and curdled milk

    I twist to rope:

Eyeing the dance of vagrant leaves—shall

    the wet grass be tied to the sky.

Whistle,

    And wait, long, until you decay:

    Tonight, when the moon shall

Come—I will sing its praises,

    and run my shadow into the far away hills.

REUNION

The knotted rope loops at the neck,

    and today, the final day, shall be

Taut the long line of rafter to floor.

    I shall not christen this a suicide,

But a birth—once more to be spat from the

    womb of nothing into the realm of nothing,

Where at least in death I shall not be known,

    in a place where her hands cannot roam.

Come with me, boy, and we shall run together.

    Perhaps, we shall find the game that you chase.

And when caught, I shall butcher it for supper.

    The raw bloody hinds will be yours,

And the gizzards, I shall stew, for me.

WILD POEMS

UNTITLED

I bed you, within a waist.
The long arched neck harkens
     among the cold yardage of snow
     within which our twin bodies
Live. Should blood lie with blood?
     Drawing forth gasps of change
     through the eyes of our skins?

JANUARY

Before man, was woman—
Before the new night—was the coldest day.
Before the window, a shroud of lace:
Veil before the face of field,
Whose stare sets upon the condensed glass
    The thighs of January.

DAYBREAK

There are only hills.

There are only trees.

There are only hills & trees:

The endless entangled twine—

The endless thickly knotted pine

 & Beyond, the anaemic shelf of slate,

& further, the endless fingers of prosrtated stone,

From the ends of which is hanged daybreak.

FIELD STUDIES

Desecrating the Field

She pressed the mango to her teeth.

The threaded fleshy pith

    jailed in youthful gaps of gums.

At the dirty feet of her lay tracks,

That had become the gavels of imperiled play.

Soon, time enough had passed throughout

The grove and the mangoes had fallen.

Softly thudding they beckoned

    roughly chapped lips

That in turn had torn apart their skins—

And nuzzled at the hidden sweetness.

IMMORTALITY

Delicious ripe soul,
    I crave.
Always, your succulent
    passion will
Our hungers indulge.

END TO AN UNPLEASANT CONVERSATION

Though after
       the
    thick light
Comes fast and
                bitter words.
    So savor
The lingering
    comfort—sweet, plump
And raw;
      Devouring the thin drizzle
        of company.

December, Adolescence

I.

The house borne in November

    Came of adolescence in December.

In the naked slur of the coldest mornings,

    laid beneath the lazy eye of white sun—

The threaded sun, a thickly spun frost would bite at her.

    And what dutiful father would not regress

To an animal savagery, to caress, between fine storms,

    the delicate awnings of her bowels. And I,

Dutiful father—would spread seed and forms of

    other dead offerings upon her toes for the dying

Birds in the afterbirth of January—all vying for a last

    supper within the shadows of daughter.

II.

Deep surgical tracts,
    hard rubbed tread had beaten—
Outcome of the act of trudging,
    round on round—incision in the ground
Of the rear lawn;
    each a knot into the earth—
& behind the rising smoke wheezing from
    the lungs of smouldering hearth,
Uttered from the cancerous phallus of chimney,
    Was forgotten—next to abandoned coffee &
Exhausted cats—dreaded work. & Under the
    ice packed hard ground rats scurried
& voles lay still—aware of the beaten dog
    that whimpered gladly in the face
Of a cold wind.

POSSIESVR

This thistle is mine:
This nectar of violet swords.
If peeled and dried—then surely
    immortality beckons.
Within the mildewed linen
    of forgotten hotel rooms would
It lay hidden. Legend spreads
    that a sleeping thistle would
Broker the birthing of a goddess.

Axle Grease

Axle grease & fact checkers.

  One,

To grease the skids of civilization
   into the arse

& one, to check it's firmly
   in there;

As if there is more to days
   then the penitent ritual

Of a prostate check over dinner—
   by sixty hours (or years)

Of overwork.

& the axle grease is dry—

The fact checkers,

        less than gentle.

COMMODITY

The Human Commodity

You are flesh

Sash upon my chest

All along the sagging boards

There are punctured worlds—

Mothered upon the hard wood

By black ten inch stilettos.

What accolades have been won

Such, is the human trophy you are:

Endless plane of body—

> The mouth fills at the estuary of your
> hips;

The craggs of your thighs

Have etched the blueprints of a premature

> pleasure upon my brow.

FIGMENTS

Beloved figment of Son,
    in the young years of your non existence
How disrespectfully at nature you have run—
    & it shall rend you.
Beloved wisp of daughter,
    still soundly kept within an unfired crucible;
Know that in my sagging years
    I have wholly loved at the feet of nature
& still often it has struck at me harshly.
    Exhausted wife—for all the years
Through which our bodies have endured,
    it is neither affection nor longing
That guides the wrath of merely being.
    Dozing upon the warm field of your
    stomach—I do not laze, but wilfully I abscond
From the reach of fingers that shall cut the wind
    from our chests regardless.

BLUE

I Do Not See the Colour Blue.

I have never seen the colour blue
Though I have realized a traumatic depth of ocean
Consume the body of a child in the gulf,
    the whole of the water a single giant unthinking maw
Opening and then just as quickly vanishing.
A vast space—sickly terrifying, where
arms, legs, and the face were eaten—slipped into
    the gut we know as blue: but I do not see it,
Nor blue elsewhere.
Gathering the crusted bodies of fruit—their sacrament
    staining my hands—sweet and moreish—
Now and then there would be one unharmed, unearthed.
Quickly wedged between a fat thumb and slim finger,
    it would be crushed, and scalp bursting would coalesce
A lace of what we know as blue—but I do
    not see,
And when the light is vanished, a multitudinous net
    of stars gathers.
Distant places where I, may also be. And there, close but far,
    their unassailable eyes are layered with a glistening film
We know as blue—but I do not see.

THE PLANTATION OF BIRDS...

The luminosity of her buttocks
  is splendid—
Roundly lunar, and behind her,
  the plantation of birds.
An oddly planetary litho—
  whereby a driven spike
Rears the constellation aviary.
   The foreground of skin and breast,
Shadows where would live the
  flit of cardinal, chickadee, and
Others alike, backs raked in a famine
  of ice—and crowns picked daily
For the guillotine of bedroom window.
   It is by night that I know the joy
of her nudity, which by moonlight is fleeting—
  but just as with my field of
Minuscule beating hearts, for now
  I shall gather what has flown.

...AND AN ACT OF MERCY

A neck forced to two hundred and seventy
Degrees—becomes triangular,
And one wonders could Pythagorean theorem
Raise the dead, untwisting the shattered bone
And blowing wind under the wings.
But pressure, you see, is a purely tangible force:
There was no hope in the small grave of snow.
The house was unflinchingly cruel, smiling
Plainly as an act of mercy was resumed.
The small mound constructed was patted down,
A rotting pick of pine was raised.

AMERICA HAS BLED ME

America has bled my wrists—and America
In bleeding them has laid bare the empty
Wash of my hollow limbs. Shells sucked of
Their juicy flesh—all remaining is the sound
Of collapsing waves, an ocean in memory.
From the cut in lieu of rivulets of blood rises
The thin waterfalls of a queer sand. If only
Sand were enough to stave the masses, would
I raise my slit wrists to their mouths—with the
Coarse sand feeding, the famished would no
Longer echo the whinnying of children's empty
stomachs. But from sand only comes a parched throat;
and had I blood left flowing in the burrows of my
heart—It would be as artificial as this land.

BREASTS

I bowed to her breasts
Then felt ashamed
Having learnt it is wrong
To covet the glamour of others.
That by wanting I can take
Without ever getting.
Then having the ill gotten
Imagined gains, I have
Imposed myself on others.
And by having taken nothing
But having an unreal something—
The transaction is off.
There are goods with no origin:
A thief with no crime.
And like that, I see, I am serving
Time for the only good thing
There is: living through the bodies
Of others—to forget my own.

I Was the Registered Owner

We wanted a dog,
And soon there was a dog
Picked from the foster house
Asleep on our floor.
A dog with a thick white coat,
A rope of fat around its neck
And one ear that stood erect,
The other perennially slumped.
On end he would bark at squirrels
And spiritedly shake his amputated
Tail when the front door beckoned,
But otherwise he would doze,
Or gaze for slow hours at nothing.
His sleep was conducted in fits,
Where waking suddenly, terrified,
He would re-position, merely to repeat.
There was no true affection apparent
In his eyes—only a languid begging
For comfort from a transparent
Disquiet. And so—we homed a dog
As broken as me. Resurrection in
His every movement of a
reenacted and terrible past—
And at night there was no sound
Enough to muffle his laboured
Breathing and no dark enough to deposit
His gently heaving shadow away.

The End

Tonight I slip into the furnace.

Bridge the cold of the house with my body.

Perhaps, then, shall a warmth engulf you.

SEEING THE FUTURE

On an undated Thursday,
In an uncertain future,
Self shackled, limbs drawn taut,
Shall be folded the human body.
Tightly, the back is to be creased,
Pressed repeatedly until failure
When will run the oil of living
And fluttering until stilled.
It shall be disappeared to residue:
A fugitive speck of man to nothing.
And in leaving—will deposit
A cold drop of bitter note
To which will be drawn everything—
Where upon approaching it,
The virgin pressed origin,
Time will reduce to a dripping pace
And the terrible cries of —
Shall resound for eternity.

MIDDLE OF A STORY

And then there came the time I lost my shoe—
It was in the middle of South Dakota,
Off the road somewhere as we rode the badlands
To Montana. I had been infatuated with the
Sweet teenage air of the big sky—and had stopped
To take a great long piss into the wide expanse,
As I had thought it was a grand idea
To drink as many warm beers, on a warm day
In a warm desert, as possible, and as I pissed my heart
Away my wife had sat immobile in the truck, and by
now I had a good idea that she was thinking about work
And not the endless distance that lay before us—
And when I had finished emptying the existence of
My soul into the upwind, I returned to the car
With half of my innards on my right shoe,
And I came to see that my left had gone and in turning
Around, I had only to glimpse it galloping into the desert
With a speed no shoe I had ever seen before possess—
Knowing it would not return. After a minute, having
Witnessed my left shoe's victorious bid for emancipation—
I hobbled into the car on my right foot, and gunning it,
We sped into the surgically folded crease of the horizon—
Thankful that I wasn't driving stick.

OLD HOUSE

Howl at me again
Damned sagging floors
Howl at the first wise guy grin
Of day that pecking moon
You jostling fools—a hundred years
You still squeeze and run
                          out of breath.
See, how my feet have yet
To know the cold vengeance of
                          winter boards,
The torment of a quick bite
And see how when they do, I am
                          in shock
And yet you howl—and howl
                          again when a man
Too early has arisen:
My bladder is my enemy,
But appears to be your friend.
                          If you could
Hush your chatter—
Lest the dependents know,
And soon the howls will come
From above and below.
Howl at me again,
                 and see
How I howl as ash shall
Blow from your cooling corpse.

FOOLISH LOVE

One does not know that they

                are dying of thirst

Until a drop of water falls upon

                the tongue.

I did not know I was rebellious

                Until you fell upon

My billowing listlessness. And then

                with a hunger,

I have opened my throat

                to let the water

Of your dissension flood my–

VILLAIN

Worship Me

Antibodies—I take yours, love. In turn, ingesting
    the plague of desire sweating from every pore,
Retching on the mist that in abundance scores the air
    around you, and they, and them, and I: you are bent.
How falteringly ungraceful, your dance—weaker by the second.
    In a sundry dress, brightly patterned and gaudy,
You play the sacrificial lamb to the altar —only priests, ignorant
And incompetent, have forgotten all sacrifices in play.
    Only who? Who I am not, sated the lust for compliance,
And then in days and years that have sped past—nothing
    could suffice. No million dead, no million tied
And forcefully bred. There was no pain great enough—the plague
    that dallied through the bread of thousands
Was the forgotten middle child of dysfunction and a languishing
    paternity. This month alone, we have bled out
Of you twenty first sons, that could have paid our way to
    the gates of paradise, which no toll would have hindered,
And the road, smooth and clean, would have laid before
    the wheels of our prayer machine. Oh, my darling
By giving the white cells that stay for today
    Your mortality you have welcomed an anguish, and that
Anguish is me. For love, for kindness, and compassion
    You have acted like a child. As foolish as the
 Indentured angels of myth, how you seat yourself among them
    on the plastic garden chairs—prettily singing,
Gazing at the congregation of one. And I have to you become god,
    and like god—shall use, demand, and conjure your body.
Occupying your drought starved plains. The rains that fall
    from you on odds days, will be because of my intervention.
That all the trinkets of worth to you, held closely, shall be weepingly
    given to me. When paid to my hands,
I shall open them, and capture the descent of your heralded objects
    falling to dirt, broken relics planted to seed a new personage.
And you shall weep, and fall sick—crying
    In regret. Where regret is all I can foster—Like the heaven that
    that is barren and unfurnished. I have taken, and will
Not give. Look back on the years—my love—as they have gone.

    And regret.

Beautiful Nose

Look at that beautiful nose—exquisitely elongated,

    A stiff little member above the quivering lip,
An erection planted on the smug face—perhaps, excited by

The galactic premise, of being, or becoming, more beautiful
    than ever.

And how one wants to touch it—to record its oscillation,
    cantilever of cartilage,

Stick two fingers up the foghorns of its intakes, and plug
    them—with pepper, with spice,

A chipolata in the steam pipe. Your beautiful eyes watering,
    the curling circling cawing men

Brandish their own erections to match yours—
    how they gallivant and light up

Pairing and parting, spreading, spitting, and struggling
    to become extravagant enough in the cosmic

Suspense, the thousandth act, overture on the constant
    reactionary orgasm. How you thrill in it,

The sea of men, mean stragglers, hooked on you,
    and that beautiful nose, deadly in a war zone, would

Flip a trip wire quicker than flick—and up would go them all,
    sizzling tuxedo tails floating feather-like in the

Goddamn wind. And there, with beer in hand, hand on heart,
    heart on the sleeve, and sleeves rolled up,

Would the kids from the local college delinquently play the tuba,
    the trumpet, the bang drum, and whistle pop—

In salute, to the men who crawled into doom,
    to get a closer look at that beautiful nose.

A Bastard, Even in My Dreams

Women are breaking my mugs—
      "YOU BASTARD"—and then–

      "YOU LOUSY FUCK", "YOU LIMP DICKED TYRANT".

      "I WANTED YOUR BABY!"

Women, in the hundreds, facilitating the

Destruction of my kitchenette. Look at them work!

      Such a team effort. It's my dream, and still they

Do want they want. I sit. In my own head. Staring

      at purple trees. Bulls with giant testicles, sweating

In the hot wind.

      A bird with hands for wings. And an army of

Women marching over the hills. Hand in hand.

      Ready to assail my porcelain goods.

"I'M PREGNANT".

"YOU KISSED THAT BITCH!"

      Oh they're yelling again. I drink my coffee out of

A vase. They've taken that too.

      I'm drinking hearty tomato soup from a boot.

It's gone.

      I sit on the bare floor of my house:

With emptiness.

LAKE POEMS

BIG LAKE

One can picture

    the rising phallus of a God-being:

Imposing and immortal—

    casting indifference, its suffocating

Shadow upon the face—eclipsing the

    Sun, Moon, and Venus,

Until all above the land—where sky should

    settle—is the flesh of its sex.

And from this sex

    comes truth—and subservience.

And from this sex—comes the fountain

    of an everlasting hope or despair.

And from this sex—billows

    the rivers of elongated birth.

LABOUR

Yet again—we suffer the supper of scuffed shoe leather.

 Cooked down only so many ways, arduously

It can be consumed—and eventually one discovers, is best

Served with a dusted field of malaise or the medicinal

 acridity of a corrosive lime soaked labour.

Both incisors were lost to the sole of an old chelsea boot

 from the now defunct steel mill.

And kindly kept—were tinned in an old mint can

 by the aged man from China whose hermitage was next door.

Hands shaking, they–teeth, were passed around in the hammered

 peppermint kept enamel—with a haranguing cloud of opium

Giving air to a scene lent operatic composition.

 In thanks, each, returned to him atop

A chipped and stained ivory salad bowl

 [the remnant pigments of a now faded cowering hare discernible

On the years rubbed surface] a slice of tannery beaten steak,

 and smiling he consumed it with is us, ferociously, in silence.

SAVAGE, SAVAGE

Under the pulpit light, see glowing
    the form of her body.
Such bountiful small breasts, and skin
    that rolls like the prairie.
Freckles dot her spine, and tumble
    down her buttocks—wildflower
Seeds in the wild paddock of her
    pressed flesh—and the fat
Which dimples, so naturally, is calling–
    the imperfection of a love for
Food, and wine. Her mouth, full
    and tender, strong enough to
Pummel the hot bones of chicken,
    and draw the juice from shattered
Dry spirits—as strong as the tide pull
    below the feet of a drowning child.
Her hair fair and broken, is wild:
    and her poise lazily savage.
A vision—of the mother of messiahs:
    her legs unshaven, and groin
Unbarred—hot, the humid foliage
    of a wild forest lives between
The thighs—and in the night,
    the forest bellows the primitive
Bell of sanctuary. Her face is broad,
    and visage many—gap toothed
And tight lipped, an expanse of thin miles—the
    tongue rolls, buoyant vessel
Among the rolling tide of saliva—
    and in the depths, her proud legs let
Flood the many dismayed lovers of
    her pest-drenched nights.

MERCURIAL SAVAGERY

THE MERCURIAL SAVAGERY OF THE MIDNIGHT ANIMAL
    IS TANGIBLE.
WHEN FACED WITH WORDS, IT LASHES OUT WITH ITS RAZOR TONGUE:
    AND FOR THIS FACT—SUBJUGATION SHALL
BE ETERNAL. RECORD THE SKIN OF THIS HAND.
    IT IS BORN OF SHIT AND INDIFFERENCE.
THE LULLABY OF MY YOUTH WAS A WHOREHOUSE IN AUCKLAND.
    THE SWEETHEART OF MY SEVENTEENTH YEAR,
WAS THE PREGNANT TEENAGE MOTHER OF A STONER'S LUST.
    AND TODAY—ON THE PISS ADDLED STREET,
"JUSTICE FOR MY DEAD LOVER"—SHE CROONS.
    SUPPING THE HARD RYE—ONE WISHES SHE WOULD
SHUT THE FUCK UP. DO YOU NOT READ—
    JUSTICE IS THE CHAIN YOU SELF IMMOLATE
WITH, AND PROTEST IS YOUR DOMINA. COME BE WANTON
    WITH A LOUSY GUTTER WORTH POET.
I SHALL SHOW YOU REDEMPTION IN MY LAUGH,
    I SHALL FEED YOU THE TALLOW OF COMPASSION
FROM MY COCK. COME SIT WITH ME—ANGERED WIDOW,
    THE SHADOW OF YOUR HUSBAND LIES IN MY CROTCH.

AFFAIR WITH MRS. GAUZE

I.

Mescalin drowned gauze—the carpet bomb prescription

       Casualties would remember, this is was the water of the baptized.

Mr. Gauze—and his celestial clinic off the sun-dried arterial interstate.

       Sleep clinic of the future—where empty dreams were vaporized.

Sleep that was merely shut your eyes, then popped from the stretched uterus

       of night into the eye burning light of six am another day—

Became ultra marathons through the desert of sexual fantasy, and repressed

       memory. And one time, Lilian was tortured for a thousand years

       straight. A half-millennia of belt whipped entrapment.

And when she woke—she fucked the brains out of Mr. Gauze, and cried out

       "Daddy!" before

       throwing herself under the Coca-Cola semi in the fast lane.

All comers to the pulpit—vagrants from 40 states—waterboarded the first

       night under the chapel of stars. Under that cool night—your trachea

Was a delight to the market of fingers (don't' think they were washed)—and the

       shit tinged soil would clot in your throat, tumbling in the

Spit of cactus, spirit of love. Some would smoke joints—and some fucked out openly.

       The desert said nothing. Quietly watching. Timekeeper—minute writer.

And the next morning, we would find some hippies twined in death, foam

       frothing from one blue tongued mouth to another. Rigor encapsulating

One groin to another. "Scorpion dive baby"—chuckled Mr. Gauze.

       Lying in the open desert air—exfoliating the days old scum from your

Back would make you cum harder than any soft bed sex—but the scorpions

       weren't messing around. So you dived, deep into the sand—and hoped you

Came up for fresh air without the sting of the black shelled hunters in

       your flesh. And Mr. Gauze, he never really spoke—catch phrases

Were really all there was. Commandments, the pure sacrament of the holy

       water—and eyes, bloodshot and ancient. Ancient, and lonely.

You can have any woman, or man. Eventually, you live through them all—

       Mr. Gauze, could tell worth from the taste of an inner thigh.

Salt lake prophecies (catch phrase #4)—vibrato of his tongue tip—flicking

    the salt from right near your cunt—salinity stiffy (catch phrase #10),

Barometer to the pressure exerted on the soul. Rarely he'd not stop licking,

    and then the world would explode with the moans from some young

Thing's unexpected resurrection.

    Mr. Gauze—neglected all—and so, neglected none. And worst off,

Was his messiah. Tortured soul of 40 years. You could see the seed of mission

    still grew. Roots of what began in the done up Airstream love machine.

But now the husk was all that blew. Mrs. Gauze. Exotic, empty. Mr. Gauze,

    lost dancing near Deimos.

Mrs. Gauze, lain naked on mornings—brush against brush of the desert.

    She kept pets on no leashes. Free to roam the desert sand.

They always came home. Such, was the flesh of her care. I always came home.

    Wonderful mistress to the lost wizard of New Mexico.

Mr. Gauze, and his Mescaline blood—Mrs. Gauze, was the wiser prophet that

    stood up on that altar. Robe slits hinting at her still alive lust.

She commanded I not partake.

    Beloved pet—my portion of flesh was ever the most bountiful.

And there, to stem the vacuum of my sleep—side effect of the

    of burden of the sober apostle.

She spoke—to pull the lips from the sleeping faces of her lovers,

So they couldn't kiss,

    but could only bite.

II.

We shall never meet!

No poems of mine shall bait you to the hook of my fingers—

      let to slide along partitions of your dimpled flesh .

No verse shall thrust you upon the sun parched

      cock, and into my waiting palms—and breasts pressed against

Sun bleached rafters, will no words

      enter you from behind—to the crash and fresh

Spit of oceanic slather. To the voyeuristic horizon, hours watching,

      we shall not swim. Your arched gate is closed to

Me. Though the sublime moss of your skin lies among the plates of

      reflected solar longing—it bathes in shade. Alexandria

Burns—and tufts of scorched parchment dither—see upon

      one how I cry for the taste of your flushed skin,

Pry the folds aside, and let me in—and as the sun sets, no words of my

      merit shall sleep. Goddess, lying still—how the inflamed city

Will gently slide into the tropic blossom of your womb.

III.

Sip the sable—sanguine curled leaf cup of night.

Cap of skull, borne to yet furnished rooms–

Sunk in the soft hips of young urns. As fragile as the ceramic

Stars kept upon top shelves, out of reach, in a grandmother's

Maze of relics—her maize field of memory.

To sip the softly warm placid lake of red currents,

To take the softly warm hands of arms swung through years.

The arborists of sunrise comes creeping gently on,

The sharp cutting clouds come to clip the night's short envy—

Like the mayfly which lives a love filled life in a day.

The night, is gone before it is even grown, and tomorrow

Will come again. Forever child-like, forever distracted.

LIFETIME MINUTES

I.

lifetime minutes—where nothing much happens.

Hours where, sure, there are breaths—and movement.

Steam clouds—storms in the baths—where naked women play:

    fat old man, groaning at the climb of stairs,

Hides his little old penis in disdain. Do not hide—old man,

    let young woman gawk, and laugh! Be proud

Of your sagging gut, and old arse. Sun spots—black checks

Against your life. The sun has loved you so, so much to

    dip its fingers in your wrinkled booklets of flesh.

Lifetime minutes—the young girl laughs. Skin silk, pubic

Forest untamed. Old man—you see how her arse dances.

    It is not for you! Your time has been—and she shall

Doze within the arms of strong young bucks.

Go—old man—and find the moon in the black puddles

    of quiet streets. Go and find the shadows of your lust

In silent peace, and perhaps then—she shall come.

II.

An albatross—glacial mariner of the seas—

    squats in the middle of the street,

Gallantly parading his wings as all speed by

    [the tips quiver ever so slightly].

Why does nobody question his dance?

Why does no one else stop to ask why?

    Why old bird do you sweep the air

Rushing from the hills, into your breast?

Why does your beak crack in the midday famine?

Here—in the bleak sun—his arms are racked until the

Sockets sing, and as I lie with him and spread my arms

    I realise how a man's fingers could never span his glory.

Here—So far from tides—there is his webbed feet,

stuck in a scratching hopscotch on the black teeth of asphalt.

Here—so far from the cool body—there is he, not a mountain bird—

So far from the tides, he attends—with no course to set,

    no ship to follow—and no film of salt

    to swab the tongues of fire from his eyes.

Why are you alone—aged albatross?

Where is your endless sea, my friend—where

Is your unfathomable freedom. Do not worry magnificent symbol—

here in the dry and broken land, I shall sit

With you, and pray—pray for an endless rain.

CONFESSIONAL

#1

All I need is one more fag; can you call it that still?
That name, or do you just rake trouble,
noose it up on the rafters in your home,
that long loud acerbic croon, even though you don't hate
    anything about the word, it rubs doom into your
Aching bruised back, muscles pulled like tensile ribbons—
all I need is a smoke. Somewhere, at some time,
I got lost, and the maps were in French, and words got tumbled,
and I couldn't talk right or talk straight, or even see the tar:
All I need is one more fag;
Dyin' man—that's what it is: I feel like the more I live, I just keep dyin',
The more I live, the more pieces they take from my puzzle.
And I keep seeing this lady, and this life, just out of reach—
At some stand, the booklet sayin ages 0-99—but passed that now, we are,
And I'm pulling skirt to infinity, and hunting—hunting for
one more fag...one more breath...and one more drink.

#2

In mornings alone I gaze, so alone I rage. Turned by the licked fingers of
Of wind through the levered frame is spun the page, the page, the empty page.
Stoic is my turtle shelled famine of company, on the lepers spit
Of unpopularity I sit. I am the one—studious and stern—who could not
Drip the ink upon the page, to blot, to smear, to spread, the blurred word
Of the testament of irk. The board of empty chairs I push and play, the backgammon of
My lonely days. It is silent when none venture to laud the camels hump
Of the two spirited heart. Who knew—I could be so detested—
Never in years have I woken rested, as it is a line, a thicket of spears
That I approach and bring to the thin fleshed ribs of my side—and like the myth
of messiah I am crucified, day upon day, to appease my fellow toilers, to cover
With the soft dirt of hours the mass graves of their fallible ways.

#3

There is a beauty cast aside the laminate butchers block of white hide,
And she is covered in the leather of an older skin, one must suppose
Still beneath the sagging weight of her now managerial indifference still
Resides the young lusting girl who once crossed the divide between the
Land one knows and the one they do not. Somewhere on a beach, spread
Thinly upon a wafer of coast—a soft cool breeze ran its tongue, ascending
The pale dimpled skin of thighs, to make camp below the fiery brush of
Her proud mount. And there, I would think, it has rested undetected for years.

#4

I have stolen from the purse of my mother—not money, but years. And now,
In my adult decades, my money cannot purchase back those hours.
Stern teachers beat into the soft pulp of our developing minds that nothing sours
When one achieves the heaven of self-entertainment. When taxes are paid,
Roads are laid, and the young pup from breeding partners swing gaily in the
Wind upon the toughened steel chains of hairy arms—all would be well. But well
Is the famished Ethiopian skipping over a silver platter of maize: fantasy
On fantasy as, I apostate, watch my mother grow old. And I was not kind as
A child, and money cannot repay the selfish adolescent sway and swagger I inflicted
Daily and nightly upon her house. I, thief who was loved, who at all points
Of the compass spun lost—could never exchange what I cannot know. To see
My own body change in hopes of redemption, only to find leaking away

The nectar of hopes.

Red, is the crescent fire—retrograde arc of her dementia,
forgetting, before her, the tremendous view from
The sky—pulpit scar across the sternum of unnamed seasons.
With forgetting, the sermons have been banded
To clear air—and the words knot in silk ties
Have spun away from her hands to the edges of groves;
Where she stands, she has stood before,
Where her feet bite into the dust and toes curl,
        the cattle has bitten first and hooves pressed.
The lands are plentiful in dirt and in death
but come fruitfully full of life at a point when rain carries
the mud on and reveals the hard flesh of women.
For want, there is nothing lacking, as hands can forever run over
the breasts of a pliant body. And in forgetting can she find,
The sapped well of renewed coming—a renewed birth.
Testament to the girth of inner beam that ensures her limbs
to be supple and yet risen, staunch against the harrowing wind:
Breath from the mouth that shrieks between trunks and
        eroded stone. Plates of bone, pressed through the
fissure of her tormented thighs—she welcomes labour,
if only to be free to take into her once more—ceded dreams.

#6

The most disappointing people, are those
Who profess their profound skills
For building relationships.
        Sculptors of the great gazing monuments
Of emotional victory. Flag fliers, whose
Hollow words flutter so valiantly in the
typhoon of human want and need—
        colours bold and fresh, seemingly
Unassailable, until the tattered thread that
Binds them to the bodies of those whom
        they cling to
Fling apart and into the turbulent sky they
Fold and disappear. Yes, they are the most
        disappointing.
And somewhere—a sodden flag lies, that no
One waves. A flag of a country that dissolved
        and ate itself. Its currency worthless,
Art uncollected, and history forgotten.
And I don't care, neither does anyone else—
        to stoop and pick it up. We walk by
As it speaks softly of its tepid demise.

#7

A two foot black racer has made home
        in the rifle barrel of a fallen oak
In the heavy relish of woods at the front door.
        And arriving home, it slips away with
Scarcely susurrant protest—its whip body
        silently driving on the grass—
                        and wild lilies .
I do not mind its predatory company;
Welcoming its carnivorous watch
        over the gateway to our isolation.
Perhaps, as the years come, we shall keep
        only the (comfort) of converging predators.

#8

Old men in Havana—dive off the shelf;
      clutch at bright fish in the carpet of
      our floor.
Cancerous lungs of disheveled typists rasp;
      the suicidal platter of sighing
journalists, one big break from notoriety and
      a fallen regime clouds the quiet dining
room. The alcoholic burst of raucous temper
Dines nightly at the hand-me-down table.
"Do not get another one this week" I am told.
But if I do not—who will save the damned
      from purgatory? And I do not mean hell
But the worse evil of having never existed
      at all.
And if I do not—how will I know that I shall
      vanish in good company?

#9

She shall love me—as they all do. Drip cloyingly
Without ever knowing her tongue is running.
It is because I do not want them to love me.
I say everything to bar that outcome. "You
Are beautiful" is an easy key. "The way shadows
Fall from your jaw—cloth upon your
Neck—how I wish to drive my tongue along
The bridge of your clavicle—long to crash my
My mouth into yours until they are one" is
Just a line. "How I want to drink your blood,
In cups, and barrels, and a flood, I want you
To river every drop of whatever is inside you
Into the gaping void of my hollow gut" is
honesty. Why they love me of all men
Is beyond comprehension. Why they suddenly
See I am not worth loving—always, on a rainy
Morning—is as well.

Hardbodied—the chest ripples
As it laughs—sucking air
At the jokes as the iris points crimp;
Lithe, smooth, set into
Skin, a bared back—gem in the prongs
Of the patina'd chair.

Net mouth spread trawling
The memory of an hour;
Suckling at the old mans sour
Jokes. Joints worn, the bearing
Of a knee at failure,
Cartilage as tea leaves circling the
Pouring points of forged mythologies.

She mouths of stars, that
Align to incur anger, or lust
Or joy, or sorrow. Tonight, I set
The thumb over the fourth star
of the greater bow: and ruined
a shirt as she bled the rage away.

Do not fall for the tongues of sweet
Girls who think affection
Comes as white doves, and
Unwilling blooms to fade, I say.
But this tongue is of earth and
Crisp lake—clear and fish borne.

It is an Earth hewn element
dug with hands in a place
The gods have grazed
—and the husk, the flecked
grit of mottled spice, softened
when drug across the
Whetstone of land
let's the fat pink muscle dance.

&

If you ask of me, what beauty is:
It is the sleds of rain driving a June mist;
It is the musky bear scrawl and broken limbs;
It is the barred owl—eyes open—sleeping;
It is the quill barbs thrown to spruce flesh;
It is the night rustle of bush mice.

It is all of these—the culminated whole,
All pressed and charged into
The palm creased tension
Of eyes come upon you when the
        face is turned.

&

If you ask of me what beauty is:

It is eyes come upon you when the
        face is turned.

The sun always rises—
today unmasks its turbulent plains
                from the
Covered face of lake

And wets its lips around
                the twining wound,
Obtusely quiet country road,
The sun is not round, instead

fleshy and tangled, spills like calico.
                It is
A mess. The heat, degenerate, from its
throat is septic—veins saffron

Stew the flags of its lips,
Fluttering the signal to advance,
onward to impale the world with
                fevered seduction;

the lines leading to

A place where there is a cure:
                medicine
For all that ails the coming me.
                And come
One further minute, I am swallowed
Whole by the engorged

borders of the morning—and am
redeemed at the feet of the soft
fleshed altar where I shall be skinned.

And hung to dry.

#12

Threatens the acrimonious storm rolled on tongues of leaves;
Above the hand hammered gravel—dire smoke;
          spit covered geese curse as they travel to paradise.
The gutters flow, the trees drip, the grass bows—
          with the excited weight of the sky.
Beneath the floral dress, she too, produces a rain—
          unlike the fresh deluge which feeds the plain,
Her pungent mist feeds only unconstrained ambition. The boughs
          have been bent as ribs, within them
Producing, the industrial churn of hearts working—emotive
          toil, is song and movement as
Her rain falls, and runs down the mask of leaves. And I, lie
          under the skies of her folded lips—paddling among the flood.

#13

The pointed silhouettes of families
Bob—targets rattled on the carriage of waves.
Perfectly agnostic of the presence
Of ours and our beasts they dive for fish
And cradle their young under the roof
            of wing.
The day they have spent quietly gathering
And come a further hour they shall begin
            their tortured roll call:
The harrowing goodnight that furrows
Between mouths of food chewed
At dusk and wine paired with the dislodging
Funereal echo of lungs busking for lungs.
            And how stupid was I to call her
My little moon—how common, how common,
How everyday the beauty of that comparison.
            How many moons are there, all greater
Than the one we have. What is so special
About the cremated husk of that lifeless rock.
            But here, is a beautiful arrow—the neck,
The body, the wing. Almost gone, almost
Forever extinguished. Still, they teeter on
            on an edge. And I am a father to them.
A terrible father, who drunkenly misses his watch.
No—no more the little moon, but little bird, red
            throated madness that has cursed my
Life to a tenacious ecstasy. Balance, ever
The gentle fold over the purgatory of those addicted
            to the flesh—and my love, there is no cure.

#14

To feel the great imposter
Floating, out on the lake water
        With me
Between the wakes of passing
        families.
Slipping under the skin—surface
Where no one can see faces.
Out there where all could ski,
Pilot the shooting boats lined up silently:
        all, except for me.
I could not stand behind the gurgling
Buoy, chase the tails of snapping
        froth,
Could only pretend to float lifelessly
In hopes to not be asked.
And now in life, I could buy the boat, buy
The skis, buy the cabin on the far lake.
Yet, I do not know how to pay
        The tariff for this privilege.
Only how to slip into the body of a woman
        as if she were a bath,
As this was the currency with which
        I was bought, and the toll with
Which I was sold.

Wild thorn in the side of her,
        pulled with the teeth;
And gathered, the red spot,
        of that dew—convalesced
Leper dropping alms on the
        On the sweat stained skin.
There is hunger, and then there
        is hunger. One is easy to
Overcome, and the other shall
        never be filled no matter
The worth of skin tied around
        the tongue.
Wild thorn in the side of her,
        pulled with the hands:
Pooled and stuffed the malleable
        dough of waist. Pulled,
And gathered her bends until the
        legs are temple pillars.
And then, only then, can the feast
        begin. A dissolution
Of any vow, to any gods, to be
        human and benevolent.

#16

Coal branded slips of skin

                                             pinched

    Through slits;
Sawdust pressed to film, until
           the manilla legs bind
And inside gestates:

        Destruction
        Pleasure
        the
               unwinding

                                      thread.

The many dissolutions
Of marriage. Where consequences are
Far
        and the flesh too near.
The shade in the lonely alley—forever
Heralds a scorned someone. Shade, like I.

My death, shall be at the hands of
        he, or many,

        and upon the tongue,
        as I am killed

Will be the scent of their failure—
The flavour, of their unraveling.

        And upon the body
        as I am spent
Will be the phantoms of their wives,
The drawings, of their unraveling.

Shade in the lonely alley—forever
Heralds, a consensual teaching.

        How rarely kitchen doors
        are locked

And a vase of wilted flowers
She had turned to whisper enter,

        the carpeted rise
        to rooms—devoid

of a thriving life. How sacred
The slabs where marriage dies,

        and upon their body
        as I till fresh seed—

        marks: the lace of where
        I have laid.

I have paved the land with the lattice
Of many ways.

Walking, to South of here—to
        Perdition:
Walking, to the house that is never,
        and always, mine.

There was a dream.
Where your hands held needles.
And tied on my skin.
Your fingers worked—and spun
    a net of wet earth.
And as you knit, I disappeared.
One breath at a time—
    the flesh was wound,
And then, when you stopped—
    It was alone.
Alone, slipped on the sweater—
it—rubbed along the soft skin
    of an untouched body,
    I was worn, never to be
washed, or discarded.

#18

I like to think that weaving
the perfect love letter
is like hand building a door
for a room in a house.

      The door means nothing.

      The room is unimportant.

      It is the person to which the door yields,
      in all moments:

      stressful,

            loving,

                  sorrowful etc.

A love letter to me is a verb.
An action.
Words can be actions can they not?
What is the my building of a door to you?

It is my encompassing affection

#19

Now—the fig sours;
                vermilion teeth, one million
In the circular mouth.
Tongue—run madly along their
Heads, run madly—parting,
                tongue fattened
                in the clear
River of arousal. Before—to lay
The eye of the fruit with the mouth
                is sweet, and delicate.

Now, to your mouth—the fig sours,
                does not compare.
                vermilion coil, one,
In the million scenes—atoned.
Thirty one years of having never
                languished in a body:

To peel the satin husk;
To peel the cotton skin;
To part the petaled face;
To part the sallow thighs;
To dip to the waiting mouth;
To dip to the waiting lips;

To be fed from the fingers of the hand:

To be fed the nectar of myself.

I Need

fingers to run a valley through....

run them through;

> to the bone,
> through flesh,
> through sinew,
> and trauma,
> calcified strata
> sorrow;

scrape the marrow from

> secrets—hollow limbs:

> light enough to float in the pond

> of your fluid—turned

> in the algae of tied hair:

fluid (that), does not mean sexual.

> fluid

but the fluid of you...
all of you....
> you the cup of wine

in which to grow both drunk

and unafraid.

AMBLING

Run through midnight—
Run through silence, encompassing:
          a shroud over the ears.
To crack the window is to invite the outside chorus in.
Prod the imagined—what it would be
          to own you—here—and then,
remember it is like all other nights
when awake, I stayed, hung over you:

          Empty pockets full of lint balls,
          ready to birth blisters,
          splinters of hair.

Hung, recording, you attenuate
to the slightest twitch,
          the lightest breath,
          come to wait for the sup of air,
the wrinkled nose—hoping to extrude fatigue
long enough to be the first thing
that is devoured in the dawn sigh.

LIFT THE COVER

Slips to bed next to you—stir, mumble, continue to sleep.
        I do not want to wake you; so peaceful, so beautifully vacant.
Run fingers to the neck, imagining light spilling over in the morning,
        hands glaze slumped shoulders, trace the constellations around your blades,
the bow pulled around the bay of ribs.
        Kiss them, again and under, lips roving over, lips wet with
want wandering over mountain-scapes of sternum, tip of tongue rushing between troughs of
cage.
        Lick the salty sleep off alabaster cloth back and drag
nails gently across myriad birth marks—each, endlessly contained.
        In the half light I see the story of your days play out in the shadows of your back.
And at each crossroad I love your skin with my wanting mouth—
        the smell of your every pore fills my nose. The way you move between breaths
captures me.
I lie behind you, and turn you over, your fingers curl to your nose,
        and it pinches in the way it does. I cannot help but kiss it. It, and your eyes,
kiss the sleep fluttering lids, lips to each, moving down your cheek to your jaw and neck.
        I lick a line, a meridian to the navel of your belly and my hands rove to your
breasts.
I summit the peaks of your hard nipples and my tongue follows,
        I descend the slopes of your breasts and my heart follows.
My gums wet with desire leech to your flesh. My fingers splay and palms grasp the waist—
        whispering wake up, I pinch and knead and pull your torso from your legs
and clasp the most tender half of you to my chest. The hair of your belly—tussock on an
endless salt plain brushes
        the harsh bristle of my cheeks, and the mist of your sex comes crawling
across the lit rink of your thighs. Dripping, you are asleep but awake,
        and with eyes closed you open yourself to me, and with eyes closed you embrace
my tongue which plays the chords of your desire,
        and with eyes closed I feast the lavish revelation of your body,
parting only once to gather leaves to wreath your mound,
        until—it is a worshiped place devoid of lust. And the moon is full and
round and bright in the sky—and paring the cleft of your soft buttocks,
        I spread and gather the wisdom of your intimacy:
dipping low to scoop my tongue like a fire bird mouthing water, I gulp the juices you discard.
        Asleep, but barely, you touch my face—and at a command,
I press forward into the warm season of your most secret paths.

I Am Ashamed

I am ashamed.

I called to make you feel better

and only inflamed the wound.

My love, my love, my little bird.

If I am your creature—forgive me my selfish ways.

For if an animal like I am gifted the touch

of a world like you then how can I at times not falter?

Know you are worth every cut I

striven to open.

I wanted to make you feel alive and wanted—

and come a day I shall.

My tongue is not always eloquent

but my voice resounds.

You are asleep now and soon will wake.

If only you were waking in this sarcophagus of mine.

I LIE - STILL NEEDS WORK

here, recording the stars crawl by,
the rotation of the cosmos ever present,
an illusion for it is we that spin,
and I wonder if I am weak and as suckling
as the worst workings of nature to you.
To realise I am not needy but roving--
and for a second moment I have found
a shard that tethers not my free spirit but
my wayward soles. I am sorry, truly, if during
this life I am to be intense and present but you,
present to me not a book but a language.
And your voice is not sound but movement,
your face not skin but a lake.
I lie both at ease and poised,
for in a breath I would kiss my way up
your legs from your feet—my mouth, teeth,
finding in each undulation reciprocity.
My nose to take in your scent, lifting it from
the papyrus of your back, wishing to inter
my face in the quarry of your clavicle and let
breath wash over me. To feel the friction of
your face on mine, and tumble with the spinning
world as I come into you, as a man—brimmed
With fallacy and adoration. Wanting to wake
you with a gentle lap of pleasure and once
awake flood you with the lahar of seed.
Your voice would not have been in vain,
that husky melt, would have blown on the forge
of my affections. To commit all sins on you which
would make your body tremble,
and all that would make the devout stutter.
You—an art I wish to to live.
And hope that come dawn, I wake to find your distant
Consumption lingering upon bare skin.

THE FINGERING THREAD

I, For You

Black pickled flowers
Sit stewing—under glass hours,
stirring, ever slightly, in the clear
        bitter mucous—splayed robes
Dangle, deceased, in between the spoon
        and long shank of stick.
Their seeds drift amiss in currents
Gently transforming skin.
        Come fall, what should have
Died, will remain, remnants stuck
        in brine—a leathered skin, and
        stamen with the pollen that never
        blew into the womb of another.
And why pickle flowers, those we shall
Not eat? Why pickle the black,
        now preserved, sheaves?
One day—they will be drained,
        pressed,
And slipped into books: opened
By children in the falls of unobserved years
        —thinking, how beautiful
The black veins of these memories,
        father—how dedicated the press
Of your fingers in the crackling flesh
        picked just for us.

CHILDHOOD

I held a balloon—stuffed of transient air,
    the homeless element frivolously
Gasped into the bladder sent skyward
    tumbling to an abyss, beyond
The scum of a stone skipped through
    a pond of nothing. And how reasonable
It is of us to take a perishable thing
    and spend it on the happiness of children.
More time than taken to make us whole,
    takes the time to make that one
Sole eye of color: and we do not blink,
    do not stutter, do not falter to gather
From the vines of rock the seeping nose
    of gas—and press, onward, to
Give it life in laughter, and the shuddering
    compress of family.

THREADS & THREADS

There is thread that ties a knot around the little
Finger, tied to the lift when sipping tea,
Or tied the sipping lips dripped in the hot waxing
Of the first shaking of sleep. A thread that does
Not need a nuanced knowledge, nor feed off
Years financed to grafting a knowing of how
To spin, and set, and slip it on the fingers: years
    we spend

Fidgeting through the daily lattice of constancy.
And at the other end—it ties to the throat. What the finger
Does the neck observes, when the hand restlessly
draws at the waist of a soft dress, the breath can
    only stutter.
On travels where the linear hills pull away, and the
Hands are left longingly at home, rested upon
    the unseeable bodies of those

We wish to carry with us but cannot tow—
That is when the thread cuts the most. It wraps
The lamps, and posts, and fences of streets,
Drags its long scraping limb through stagnant rain,
Mars the paint of antique facades, and catches upon
The thrusting tangle of bushes and ornamental trees.
    In the Americas, they speak of the thread in
Spiritual terms—an animal, perhaps a bird, that

    circles and caws, seemingly ever vigilant
For the moment we disregard its presence, and then
    only then,
Will it descend. In the East, I have heard told
It is as a pungent smoke, a herb cindered, an incense set,
To scent the way—once, a lonely widow in a teeming
    stall told of how she could smell the
lingering neckline of her long dead husband inches

    from her face—always, and on days of rain
Smell the drip of fresh sky pooling at his clavicle.
This myth is borne across the world,
    in towns that never know that else exists.
The thread is wound far along the shadows cast
    by sun—and shall be wound until the all the
Days and nights are run through and hollow
And cast aside.

I saw a casket, once, open with a still
Cold death cradled within—and on the hand
That crossed the top most point of the chest,
    was a looped string. The thread still wound
Even when the body stills and does not sing.
I wonder, what becomes of the threaded buried millions?
    What becomes of the net that scores the soil beneath
The streets? What shall become of me—when

Gone? Shall the longing I posses resound?

BRUTE/STONE

The mountain rounds like bones of a child
Who perished in growth
And so, seemingly, it looms ever higher.
The summit ridge, broken treeline,
    and balding scalp of wearied stone collect
Like the humped spine of a divinely prostrate
adolescence—and we scramble and claw, slip on the now
Icing dew, only hours after waking. Yawning and tumbling
In retreat, a few steps   to then reach and draw.
    This effort, vigorous and inhumane, leads to the crest
of the haggard back— to end, straddling moss haired crop,
    lazily fingering the fern hairs at the feet,
gazing down triumphantly at the limpid arms slipping
without life to the cinched waist of the Connecticut,
    submerged fingers toying the silt
Thighs of that slowly winding brute, coiling onward
    out of sight: coiling onward relentlessly—all the world
Roving sluggishly.

About the Author

D. Mars Yuvarajan: Tamil New Zealand poet. Born: United Kingdom. Adopted: New Zealand [1995]. Degrees Held: BEng [Mechanical], M.C.W.[Poetry].

Lightning Source UK Ltd.
Milton Keynes UK
UKHW041830190822
407575UK00008B/169/J